First published in this edition in 2014 by Buster Books, an imprint of Michael O'Mara
Books Limited, 9 Lion Yard, Tremadoc Road, London SW4 7NQ

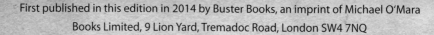 www.busterbooks.co.uk
Buster Children's Books
@BusterBooks

© 2014 by geobra Brandstätter GmbH & Co. KG

® PLAYMOBIL "pronounced: plāy-mō-bēēl"

www.playmobil.com

Licensed by: BAVARIA SONOR, Bavariafilmplatz 7, D-82031 Geiselgasteig

A CIP catalogue record for this book is available from the British Library.

ISBN: 978-1-78055-302-3

2 4 6 8 10 9 7 5 3 1

Papers used by Buster Books are natural, recyclable products
made from wood grown in sustainable forests. The manufacturing processes
conform to the environmental regulations of the country of origin.

This book was printed in May 2014 by Shenzhen Wing King Tong
Paper Products Co., Ltd., Shenzhen, Guangdong, China.

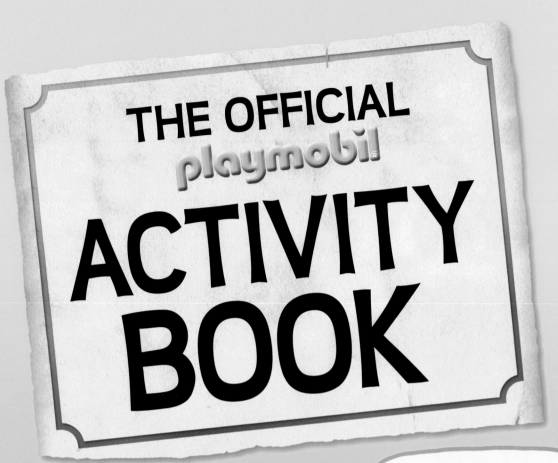

THE OFFICIAL
playmobil®
ACTIVITY
BOOK

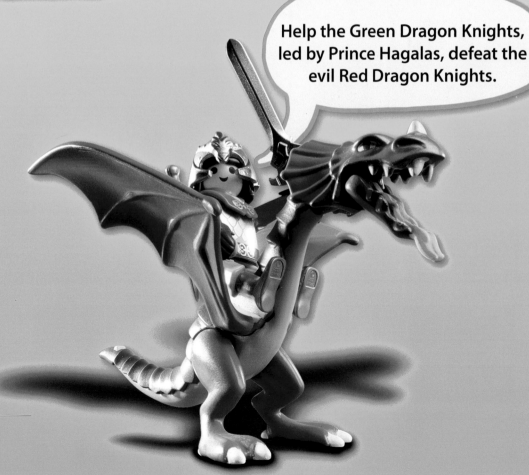

Help the Green Dragon Knights, led by Prince Hagalas, defeat the evil Red Dragon Knights.

Code Cracker

Can you write the names of the four numbered objects in the boxes below?
Then crack the code by making a new word from the letters in the yellow boxes.
Check your answers on page 62.

1 ☐☐☐☐

2 ☐☐☐☐

3 ☐☐☐☐☐☐☐

4 ☐☐☐☐

CODEWORD: ☐☐☐☐☐

Castle Colouring

Oh no! Prince Hagalas has fallen through a secret trapdoor in the Red Dragon Knights' castle. Add colour to bring the picture to life.

Silhouette Spotter

The Red Dragon Prince is ready for battle! Can you spot which of the silhouettes below matches the picture on the right? Check your answer on page 62.

DID YOU KNOW?

The Red Dragon Prince is an expert swordsman. Only the very best knights in the land can beat him.

1

2

3

4

5

A Secret Message

Sorcerer Runestone is helping the Green Dragon Knights. He has hidden a secret message for them on the parchment below.

Can you help the knights work out the message, before the evil Red Dragon Knights do?

X	Y	D	G	Z	X	D	Q	R	J	B	L	L
T	R	M	E	E	T	U	N	K	T	X	P	P
X	X	R	R	S	T	A	Z	X	S	P	Z	L
Y	T	H	E	L	X	T	S	Z	M	R	X	Y
X	S	Y	C	Y	S	H	X	Y	V	X	S	Z
W	T	G	X	B	M	X	V	X	L	K	H	X
X	Y	Z	Y	I	X	N	Y	G	V	X	Y	R
W	G	R	O	G	S	E	N	X	Z	N	N	X
R	X	Z	Y	S	Q	X	R	P	M	R	X	L
W	S	D	R	A	G	O	N	B	Z	K	F	Q
F	R	B	C	M	E	N	T	O	W	E	R	G
G	Y	Z	T	T	X	R	Y	S	X	D	Y	Q

Find the following words, which are hidden in the wordsearch. Check your answers on page 62.

DRAGON   TOWER
THE   AT
MEET

Once you've found the words, put them in the correct order to create a secret message and write it below.

SECRET MESSAGE:

Dot To Dot

Join the dots from 1 to 96 to create a fantastic, fire-breathing dragon.

Rhyme Time

The court jester, who speaks only in rhyme, has sent this scroll to the Green Dragon Prince, but there are some words missing. Can you choose the correct word to complete each sentence? The rhymes should help you fill some of the gaps.
Check your answers on page 62.

1. The Green Dragon Prince is the noblest ruler of them all.

2. His armour shines like crystal and his horse will never _____ .

3. He locks enemies in his _____ with thick walls made of stone.

4. Then he flies with his _____ to sit upon his _____ .

dungeon

throne

fall

dragon

Code Cracker

Can you write the names of the four numbered objects in the boxes below?
Then crack the code by making a new word from the letters in the yellow boxes.
Check your answers on page 62.

1

2

3

4

CODEWORD:

10

Catapult Colouring

The Green Dragon Knights have built a catapult in the woods.
Colour in the scene.

Jigsaw Jumble

The Dragon Knight jigsaw is nearly complete ... but can you decide where the missing pieces should go? Check your answers on page 62.

Out Of Place

Beneath this picture of the Great Dragon Castle there are 13 different objects. Four of them do not appear in the picture – can you circle them? Look carefully, the objects may be well hidden. Check your answers on page 62.

Spot The Difference

PICTURE 1

DID YOU KNOW?

Prince Hagalas and his faithful knights often practise fighting together. They're always careful not to hurt each other, though.

Both of these pictures show the Green Dragon Knights with their catapult. Spot the five differences in the second picture and circle them, then check your answers on page 62.

PICTURE 2

Can You Spot?

The magnifying glass shows a small section of an object in the image above. Can you work out what it is? Write your answer below.

ANSWER:

Puzzle

Silhouette Spotter

Can you match the correct silhouette to this picture of Sorceror Runestone and his magic staff? Check your answer on page 62.

Check your answer on page 62.

DID YOU KNOW?

Sorceror Runestone has a powerful magic staff. It contains the force of the Fire Dragon.

1

2

3

4

5

Colour By Numbers

Follow the colour code at the bottom of the page to colour
and complete this fearsome Dragon Knight.

1 GREY **2** RED **3** BROWN **4** LIGHT GREEN

5 DARK GREEN **6** BLACK **7** LIGHT BLUE

17

Spot The Difference

PICTURE 1

There are seven differences between these two pictures of the Green Dragon's lair.
Can you spot them all? Check your answers on page 62.

PICTURE 2

Silhouette Spotter

The Red Fire Dragon is flying across the land. But which of the five silhouettes below is his? Check your answer on page 62.

DID YOU KNOW?

The powerful Red Fire Dragon is known for hunting sheep. That is why he is so unpopular with farmers.

1

2

3

4

5

A Mounted Knight

Can you complete the drawing of the knight and his horse using the finished picture below as a guide?

TIP:
Look closely at the small finished picture, and try to copy the lines, one little box at a time.

A Secret Message

Sorcerer Runestone has written a second secret message for his Green Dragon Knights. Find the following words, which are hidden in the wordsearch.

DRAGON   RED
LET   US
ATTACK   THE

X	Y	L	E	T	O	W	T	E	X	F	S	P	X
U	S	G	X	H	Y	R	P	X	Z	P	P	P	C
S	L	R	R	S	T	Z	X	Y	S	P	Z	L	T
T	J	A	T	T	A	C	K	Y	M	R	O	A	X
X	Y	I	C	A	S	T	I	Z	V	X	S	Z	V
W	S	F	R	O	X	H	R	Q	L	K	H	U	G
X	Y	E	N	N	X	E	X	G	V	D	E	N	V
R	S	N	E	T	R	F	S	R	Z	N	N	X	R
E	X	Y	L	S	X	E	R	O	T	E	N	L	G
D	R	D	R	A	G	O	N	U	R	S	T	E	N
T	J	K	K	D	O	S	V	Q	T	K	L	G	G
R	D	M	B	P	X	R	Y	S	X	X	A	N	C

Once you've found the words, put them in the correct order to create a secret message and write it below. Check your answers on page 62.

SECRET MESSAGE:

Dot To Dot

Join the dots from 1 to 82 to reveal this brave Dragon Knight.

23

Code Cracker

Can you write the names of the four numbered objects in the boxes below?
Then crack the code by making a new word from the letters in the yellow boxes.
Check your answers on page 62.

1

2

3

4

CODEWORD:

24

Dungeon Escape

Prince Hagalas is escaping from the dungeon in the Red Dragon Knights' castle.
Colour in the scene.

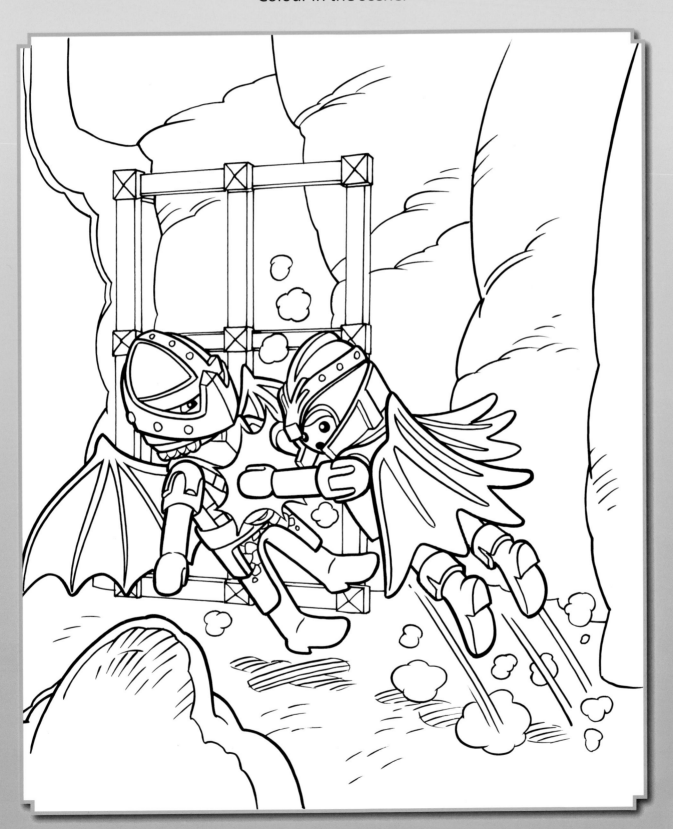

Word Finder

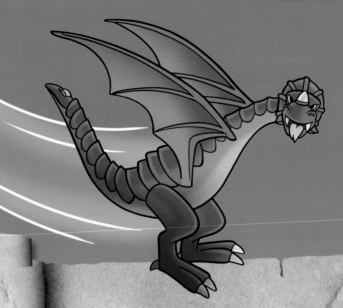

On the parchment scroll below is a letter Prince Hagalas has written to a friend. However, the message has got wet, and some words have become blurred. Fill in the correct words, choosing from the options below. Check your answers on page 62.

The Red _____ is planning an attack _____. All Green Dragon _____ must gather straight away. We must think of a plan to _____ the _____ against the forces of the Red Dragon.

Dragon

defend

Knights

tower

tonight

Dragon Drawing

Can you complete the drawing of this fearsome dragon
using the finished picture below as a guide?

TIP:
Look closely at the
small finished picture,
and try to copy the lines
one little box at a time.

Spot The Difference

PICTURE 1

DID YOU KNOW?

Many dragons have strongholds where they hide treasure. Some knights know about these secret hiding places, and fight each other while trying to steal the treasure.

There are five differences between these two pictures of the dragon guarding its treasure. Can you spot them all? Check your answers on page 62.

PICTURE 2

Can You Spot?

The magnifying glass shows a close up of a part of the image above. Can you work out what it is? Write your answer below.

ANSWER:

Dragon Maze

The green dragon wants to find his friend, the blue dragon.
Use a pencil to help him find the right path. Check your answer on page 62.

Castle Crossword

Can you solve this crossword puzzle? Write your answer to each question in the correct boxes below. When you have finished, unscramble the six letters in the blue boxes to make the codeword at the bottom of the page. Check your answers on page 62.

Across:
1. What did Prince Hagalas fall through when he was captured by the Red Dragon Knights? (8)
2. Which defensive weapon can hurl heavy stones at the enemy? (8)
   The Knights are friendly with this kind of flying beast. (6)

Down:
1. What animal does a knight ride? (5)
2. Prince Hagalas is a Green … (6,6)
3. What does a knight wear for protection in battle? (6)
4. When on horseback, most knights carry a … to ward off blows. (5)

CODEWORD:

Code Cracker

Can you write the names of the four numbered objects in the boxes below?
Then crack the code by making a new word from the letters in the yellow boxes.
Check your answers on page 62.

1

2

3

4

CODEWORD:

Combat Colouring

The Red Dragon Prince is attacking Hagalas with his lance.
Can you add colour to bring the picture to life?

Word Finder

Some letters are missing from the words under the pictures below. Can you fill the gaps to make full words? The letters at the bottom of the page will help. Check your answers on page 62.

R | | | | T | O | N | E   C | A | T | | | | T

S | | | | G | H | O | L | D   D | | | | O | N

UNGE - APUL - UNES - TRON

Castle Counting

How many of each of the objects at the bottom of the page can you spot on the parchment? Count them up then put a number under each picture. Check your answers on page 62.

35

Jigsaw Jumble

The Green Dragon Knight jigsaw is nearly complete ... but can you decide where the missing pieces should go? Check your answers on page 62.

Secret Message

B	E	H	M	T	X	D	Q	X	H	F	S	P
E	S	G	X	H	T	E	P	X	Z	P	P	P
W	L	O	F	X	T	U	C	H	X	P	Z	L
A	J	R	S	L	H	C	S	V	M	R	Y	X
R	Y	R	C	X	E	H	I	O	V	X	S	Z
E	S	G	H	Z	X	X	F	I	E	R	Y	X
X	Y	M	N	N	X	N	Y	G	V	A	Y	R
W	S	S	X	R	E	D	X	R	Z	V	N	X
R	X	U	L	S	A	E	R	P	M	R	O	L
D	R	A	G	O	N	N	F	A	N	Z	E	X
B	I	R	G	D	X	S	V	Q	T	K	L	G
G	N	Z	T	T	X	R	L	A	N	C	E	X

Here is Sorcerer Runestone's third secret message to the Green Knights. Can you find the following words, which are hidden in the wordsearch? Check your answer on page 63.

LANCE   OF
THE   DRAGON
FIERY   RED
BEWARE

DID YOU KNOW?

The Red Dragon Prince sometimes rides an armoured warhorse and uses a fiery red dragon lance when going into battle.

Once you've found the words, put them in the correct order to create a secret message and write it below.

SECRET MESSAGE:

37

Out Of Place

Around this picture of the Great Dragon Castle you can see nine different objects. Three of them do not appear in the picture – can you circle them? Check your answers on page 63.

Jigsaw Jumble

This jigsaw of the Red Dragon Knight is nearly complete … but can you decide where the missing pieces should go? Check your answers on page 63.

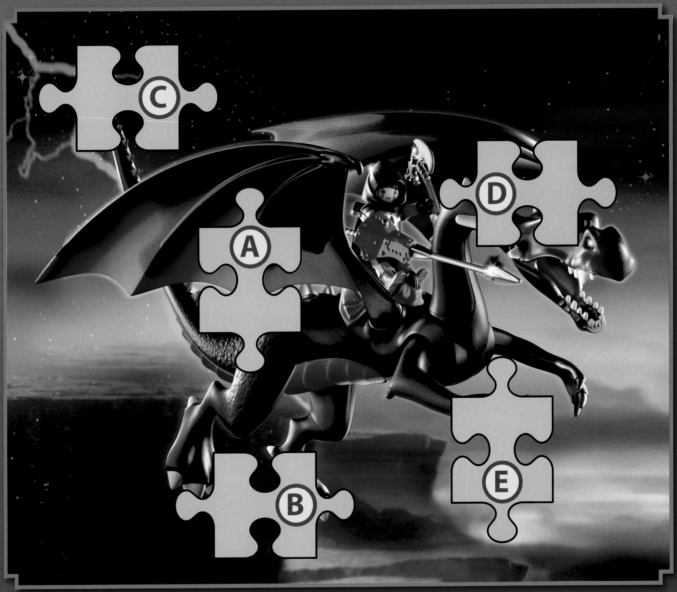

Code Cracker

Can you write the names of the four numbered objects in the boxes below?
Then crack the code by making a new word from the letters in the yellow boxes.
Check your answers on page 63.

1 ☐☐☐☐☐

2 ☐☐☐☐☐☐

3 ☐☐☐☐☐

4 ☐☐☐☐☐☐☐☐

CODEWORD: ☐☐☐☐☐☐

Flight Of The Dragon

The Green Dragon is on his way to the Red Dragon Prince.
Add colour to bring this picture to life.

Super Search

Beneath this picture of the Red Dragon Knights' Castle are pictures of four objects. Can you find and circle them in the main picture? Check your answers on page 63.

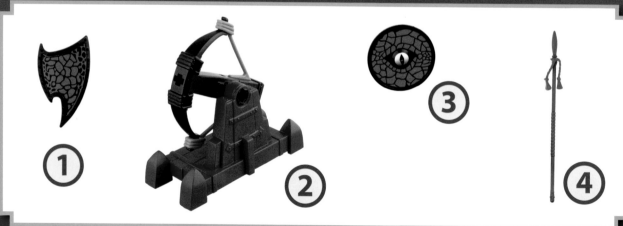

Silhouette Spotter

Which of the five silhouettes below exactly matches that of the Red Dragon Knight in the picture? Check your answer on page 63.

1

2

3

4

5

43

Spot The Difference

PICTURE 1

The castle of the Red Dragon Knights is guarded by a powerful dragon. To protect the fortress from intruders, the drawbridge is almost always closed. Inside the tower is a very powerful crystal called Dragon Light.

Puzzle

There are five differences between these two pictures of the Red Dragon Knights' Castle. Can you spot them all? Check your answers on page 63.

PICTURE 2

Can You Spot?

The magnifying glass shows a small section of an object in the image above. Can you work out what it is? Write your answer below.

ANSWER:

45

Dot To Dot

Join the dots from 1 to 94 to reveal a knight riding a fire-breathing dragon!

DID YOU KNOW?

The dragon Horgh has been a slave of the Red Dragon Knights for centuries. They have bewitched him so that he is under their spell and must always do their bidding.

Secret Message

X	Y	B	R	I	N	G	T	X	H	F	S	P
W	S	G	X	H	T	R	P	X	Z	P	P	P
E	L	L	A	J	T	X	R	X	S	P	Z	L
A	J	R	T	O	X	T	S	X	M	R	Y	X
P	Y	R	L	Y	S	H	X	Y	V	X	S	Z
O	S	G	E	X	X	E	A	F	F	E	N	Y
N	Y	M	X	N	X	N	Y	G	V	X	Y	R
S	M	I	T	X	M	E	E	T	I	N	G	X
R	X	X	L	S	X	Y	R	Z	M	R	X	L
W	S	L	L	L	S	L	S	U	Z	K	F	Q
Y	X	Q	X	D	X	S	V	M	T	K	L	G
T	R	E	F	F	P	U	N	P	L	A	C	E

Hidden on this parchment is Sorcerer Runestone's fourth secret message. Find the following words, which are hidden in the wordsearch. Check your answers on page 63.

PLACE   TO
BRING   MEETING
THE   WEAPONS

Once you've found the words, put them in the correct order to create a secret message and write it below.

SECRET MESSAGE:

Code Cracker

Can you write the names of the four numbered objects in the boxes below?
Then crack the code by making a new word from the letters in the yellow boxes.
Check your answers on page 63.

1

2

3

4

CODEWORD:

Dragon Colouring

In the picture below, the Green Dragon is coming to the aid of his friend, Prince Hagalas. Colour in this scene.

Silhouette Spotter

Which of the five silhouettes below exactly matches that of the Great Dragon Castle? Check your answer on page 63.

Dragon Maze

The Red Dragon Prince has lost some shields in this cloud maze. Each entrance to the maze is shown by a number. Can you help him pick the right path? Check your answer on page 63.

Rhyme Time

The court jester is back with another rhyming scroll. Help Prince Hagalas decipher it by adding the correct rhyming words to the text from the options at the bottom of the page. Check your answers on page 63.

1. Walking through the forest, I saw a knight.
   With him was a dragon, ready to _____.

2. He held a shield and a tall _____;
   He stood firm with a brave and fearsome stance.

3. At his feet was a pile of _____,
   Taken from a dragon's stronghold.

4. He looked at me, and I cowered in fright.

5. Until he said: 'Don't worry, I'm a Green Dragon _____!'

Knight

lance

fight

gold

A Brave Dragon Knight

Can you complete this drawing of a Dragon Knight
using the finished picture below as a guide?

TIP:
Look closely at the
small finished picture,
and try to copy the lines,
one little box at a time.

Word Scramble

Below are five words – but all of the letters have been scrambled! Can you un-scramble them and write the real words in the boxes? Check your answers on page 63.

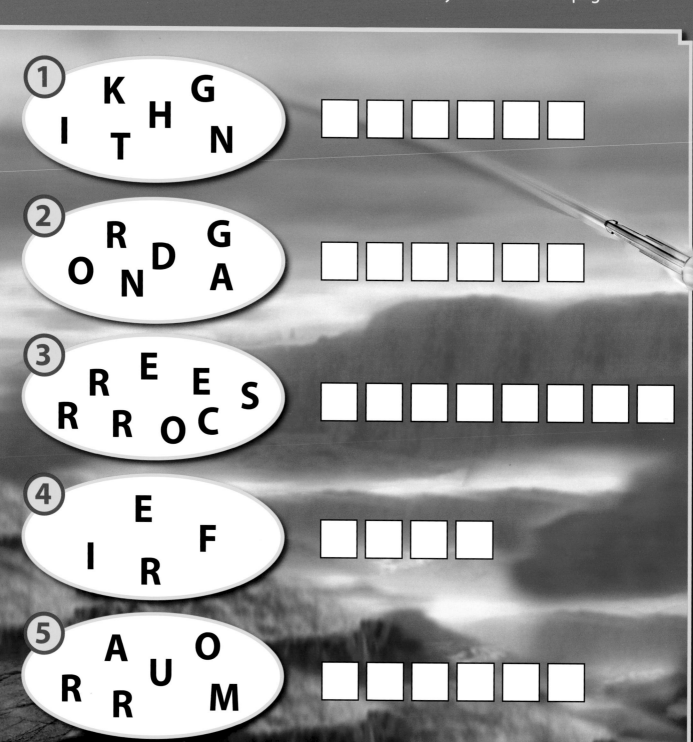

1. K H G I T N

2. R D G O N A

3. R E E S R R O C

4. E F I R

5. A O R U M R R

Secret Message

Hidden in the parchment below is Sorcerer Runestone's fifth secret message. Find the following words, which are hidden in the wordsearch.

MIDNIGHT	TO
AT	RIVER
THE	COME

Once you've found the words, put them in the correct order to create a secret message and write it below the parchment. Check your answers on page 63.

C	O	M	E	T	X	D	Q	X	Z	X	Z	R
W	S	X	Y	H	T	R	P	Z	Z	P	F	I
O	X	U	T	H	E	X	R	Y	S	P	Z	V
O	J	M	X	L	X	C	S	X	M	R	Y	E
X	Y	X	C	X	S	H	X	X	V	X	S	R
T	A	T	H	M	R	N	A	C	H	T	X	Y
O	Y	X	N	N	X	N	Y	G	V	X	Y	R
W	S	Z	X	T	A	T	S	R	Z	N	N	X
R	X	U	L	S	X	Y	R	P	M	R	X	L
W	S	M	L	L	F	L	U	S	S	K	Z	Z
B	X	Y	G	D	X	S	V	Q	T	K	Z	Z
M	I	D	N	I	G	H	T	S	X	D	Y	Q

SECRET MESSAGE:

Code Cracker

Can you write the names of the four numbered objects in the boxes below?
Then crack the code by making a new word from the letters in the yellow boxes.
Check your answers on page 63.

1

2

3

4

CODEWORD:

Returning Home

The Green Dragon Knights and their dragon are on their way home.
Colour in the scene.

Jigsaw Jumble

The Red Dragon Knight jigsaw is nearly complete … but can you decide where the missing pieces should go? Check your answers on page 63.

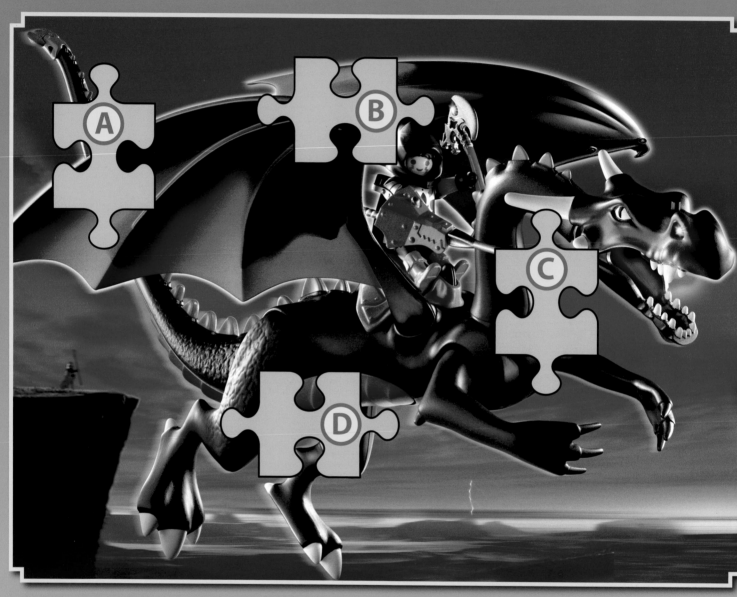

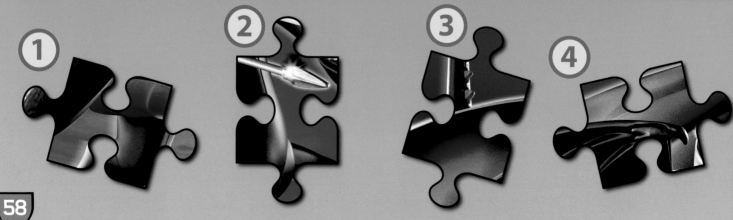

Crossword Chaos

Can you solve this crossword puzzle? Write your answer to each question in the correct boxes below. When you have finished, unscramble the six letters in the blue boxes to make the codeword at the bottom of the page. Check your answers on page 63.

Across:
1. Dragons store this in their lairs. (8)
2. The part of a castle in which prisoners are held. (7)
3. The Dragon Light … is kept in the Red Dragon Knights' castle. (7)
4. This is the tallest part of a castle. (5)

Down:
1. What kind of building do the Dragon Knights live in? (6)
2. What does a knight wear on his head to protect him? (6)
3. The magician's name is Sorcerer … (9)
4. Knights fight hand-to-hand with this weapon. (5)

CODEWORD:

59

Dragon Knight Quiz

1. **Who rides the Red Dragon?**
   - A Prince Hagalas
   - B The Red Dragon Prince
   - C The Green Dragon Knights

2. **Which of these can a dragon NOT do?**
   - A Breathe fire
   - B Fly
   - C Read

3. **How many towers does the Great Dragon Castle have?**
   - A Two
   - B Five
   - C Nine

4. **Who lives in the Great Dragon Castle?**
   - A The Red Dragon Knights
   - B The Green Dragon Knights
   - C The country folk

5. **What is on the gate of the Great Dragon Castle?**
   - A The head of a chicken
   - B The head of a frog
   - C The head of a dragon

6. **What is a dungeon?**
   - A A kitchen
   - B A prison
   - C A concert hall

You're well on your way to becoming a real Dragon Knight, so the following quiz should be easy! Check your answers on page 63.

7. **What is hidden in the tower of the Red Dragon Knights?**
- **A** The Dragon Light Crystal
- **B** A dragon egg
- **C** A dragon child

8. **How do Dragon Knights fire their fireballs?**
- **A** With a cannon
- **B** With a shotgun
- **C** With a catapult

9. **What is the real name of the Sorcerer?**
- **A** Ranlow
- **B** Rumpleton
- **C** Runestone

10. **What gives the Sorcerer his powers?**
- **A** His magic scroll
- **B** His magic staff
- **C** His magic saucepan

11. **Who is the Sorcerer fighting against?**
- **A** The Red Dragon Knights
- **B** The Green Dragon Knights
- **C** The Pink Dragon Knights

 Answers

Page 4   boot, wing, helmet, door
              Codeword: tower
Page 6   Silhouette 3 is correct.
Page 7

X	Y	D	G	Z	X	D	Q	R	J	B	L	L
T	R	M	E	E	T	U	N	K	T	X	P	P
X	X	R	R	S	T	A	Z	X	S	P	Z	L
Y	T	H	E	L	X	T	S	Z	M	R	X	Y
X	S	Y	C	Y	S	H	X	Y	V	X	S	Z
W	T	G	X	B	M	X	V	X	L	K	H	X
X	Y	Z	Y	I	X	N	Y	G	V	X	Y	R
W	G	R	O	G	S	E	N	X	Z	N	N	X
R	X	Z	Y	S	Q	X	R	P	M	R	X	L
W	S	D	R	A	G	O	N	B	Z	K	F	Q
F	R	B	C	M	E	N	T	O	W	E	R	G
G	Y	Z	T	T	Z	R	Y	S	X	D	Y	Q

              Secret message: Meet at the
              Dragon Tower.
Page 9   The words fit in the following
              order: fall, dungeon, dragon, throne.
Page 10   sword, tree, arrow, rock
              Codeword: star
Page 12   1 E – 2 C – 3 B – 4 D – 5 A
Page 13

Pages 14 –15

              Answer: shield
Page 16   Silhouette 1 is correct.
Pages 18 – 19

Page 20   Silhouette 5 is correct.
Page 22

X	Y	L	E	T	O	W	T	E	X	F	S	P	X
U	S	G	X	H	Y	R	P	X	Z	P	P	P	C
S	L	R	R	S	T	Z	X	Y	S	P	Z	L	T
T	J	A	T	T	A	C	K	Y	M	R	O	A	X
X	Y	I	C	A	S	T	I	Z	V	X	S	Z	V
W	S	F	R	O	X	H	R	Q	L	K	H	U	G
X	Y	E	N	N	X	E	X	G	V	D	E	N	V
R	S	N	E	T	R	F	S	R	Z	N	N	X	R
E	X	Y	L	S	X	E	R	O	T	E	N	L	G
D	R	D	R	A	G	O	N	U	R	S	T	E	N
T	J	K	K	D	O	S	V	Q	T	K	L	G	G
R	D	M	B	P	X	R	Y	S	X	X	A	N	C

              Secret message: Let us
              attack the Red Dragon.
Page 24   ground, wing, helmet, hand
              Codeword: gold
Page 26   The words fit in the following
              order: Dragon, tonight,
              Knights, defend, tower.
Pages 28 – 29

              Answer: treasure
Page 30   Route 4 is correct.
Page 31

```
              ³A
               R
               M
               O
               U
¹T R A P ²D O O R
        R
      ²C A T A P U L ⁴T
        A          A
        G          N
        O          C
        N          E
      ¹H K
       O N
       R I
       ³D R A G O N
       S H
       E T
```

              Codeword: heroic
Page 32   sky, lance, horse, torch
              Codeword: track
Page 34   runestone, catapult,
              stronghold, dungeon
Page 35

              6   7   5   9   4   8

Page 36   1 C – 2 D – 3 B – 4 A